Leaders in the Texas Revolution

United for a Cause

Kelly Rodgers

Consultant

Julie Hyman, MS.Ed.
Social Studies Coordinator
Birdville ISD

Publishing Credits

Dona Herweck Rice, *Editor-in-Chief*
Lee Aucoin, *Creative Director*
Marcus McArthur, Ph.D., *Associate Education Editor*
Neri Garcia, *Senior Designer*
Stephanie Reid, *Photo Editor*
Rachelle Cracchiolo, M.S.Ed., *Publisher*

Image Credits:

Cover Bridgeman Art Library & State Preservation Board, Austin, Texas; pp.2–3 State Preservation Board, Austin, Texas; p.4 Bridgeman Art Library; p.5, 6 The Granger Collection; p.7 Bridgeman Art Library; p.8 Texas State Library and Archives Commission; p.9 (top) Greg Ward/Flicrk; p.9 (bottom) Bridgeman Art Library; p.10 Texas State Library and Archives Commission; p.11 Declaration of Independence of the Republic of Texas (1836), via Google books; p.12 Texas State Library and Archives Commission; p.13 (top) The Granger Collection; p.13 (bottom) Bridgeman Art Library; p.14 Getty Images; pp.14–15 Corbis; p.16 Newscom; p.17 The Granger Collection; p.18 (left) Texas State Library and Archives Commission; p.19 Bridgeman Art Library; p.20 Alamy; p.22, 23 Bridgeman Art Library; p.24 State Preservation Board, Austin, Texas; pp.24–25 Getty Images; p.26, 27 Bridgeman Art Library; p.28 The Texan Emigrant by Edward Stiff (1840), Public Domain; p.29 San Jacinto Museum; p.32 Alamy; All other images Shutterstock.

Teacher Created Materials
5301 Oceanus Drive
Huntington Beach, CA 92649-1030
http://www.tcmpub.com

ISBN 978-1-4333-5047-4

Printed in China WAI002

Table of Contents

Gone to Texas

During the early 1800s, Mexico invited Americans to settle in Texas. At the time, Texas was part of Mexico. It was called *Tejas* (TAY-has) in Spanish. Mexico hoped the settlers would make northern Mexico more successful. And they hoped the settlers would keep it safe from American Indian attacks.

Because life was hard in the United States, many Americans moved to Texas. Some took their slaves with them. Mexican-born settlers moved to Texas, too. But by 1830, most of the people who lived in Texas had come from the United States.

Mexican leaders passed laws that made it illegal for Americans to move to Texas. They were worried that there were too many Americans in Texas. Mexico passed other laws that forced Americans to pay more taxes and give up their slaves.

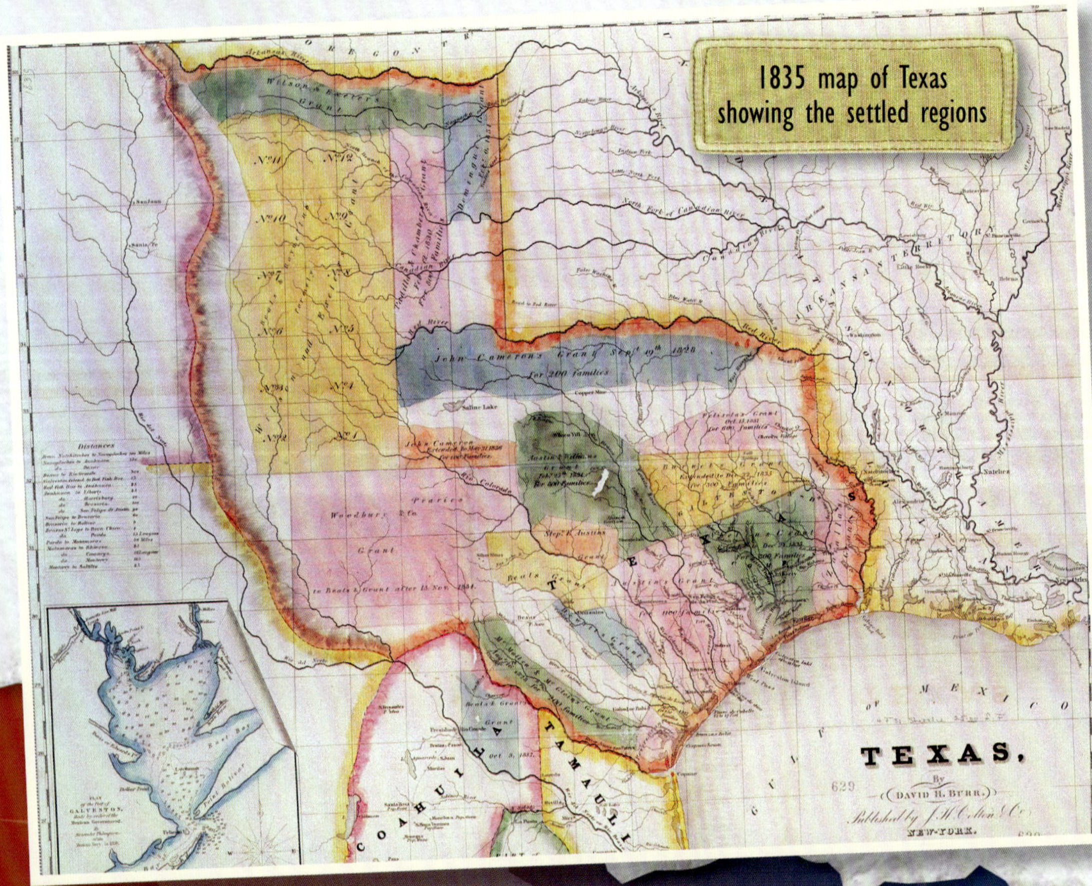

1835 map of Texas showing the settled regions

the Battle of the Alamo during the Texas Revolution

The Texas settlers grew angry. The people of Texas wanted to be free from Mexico and felt Texas should be able to make its own laws. In 1835, a **revolution** began. **Texians** (TEK-see-uhnz) fought for their independence, or freedom. Men and women played important roles in the struggle. Their courage tells the story of the Texas Revolution.

What Is a Revolution?

The word *revolution* means that a great change has taken place. Some revolutions involve warfare. The American Revolution was a time when people living in America fought to break free from Great Britain. The Americans formed their own government. The Texas Revolution involved Texas settlers fighting for independence from Mexico.

Revolutions are not always bloody wars. The Industrial Revolution was a time when people began to use machines to replace the work of men. The Scientific Revolution was a time of great intellectual change and scientific advance.

Legendary Leaders

Stephen F. Austin and Sam Houston

Stephen F. Austin and Sam Houston were leaders of **colonization** in Texas. They were also leaders in the Texas Revolution.

In many ways, Austin and Houston had similar lives. Both were born in Virginia in 1793. They studied law and served in the military. They also both held political offices.

Austin became an **empresario** (im-press-AHR-ee-o). In 1822, he settled the first American colony in Texas. When the revolution broke out in 1835, Austin supported independence for Texas. He led troops into battle. He also worked to get military support from the United States. Later, Austin tried to make Texas part of the United States. He did not live to see this happen. Austin died in 1836.

U.S. stamp honoring the 100-year anniversary of the Republic of Texas

Houston and his men charge the Mexican lines.

Houston came to Texas in the 1830s. In 1836, he became major general of the Texian Army. Houston led the attack at San Jacinto (sahn ha-SEEN-toh). It was there that Texas won its independence by defeating the Mexican Army.

Houston served as the first president of the Republic of Texas. When Texas joined the United States, Houston served as a U.S. senator. He later became the governor of Texas.

Empresarios

When Mexico won its freedom from Spain in 1821, it invited Americans to settle in Texas. Mexico gave settlers, or empresarios, land in Texas. Empresarios were in charge of getting more Americans to settle on their Texas land.

The Old 300

In 1821, Moses Austin, Stephen F. Austin's father, got permission from the Mexican government for 300 families to move to Texas. Moses died before he was able to move to Texas. Austin decided to carry out his father's plan. The original 300 families who settled in Austin's Colony were known as *the Old 300*.

Revolutionary Writers

George Childress

George Childress

Many of the settlers in Texas came seeking a new life. This was true for George Childress. Childress grew up in Tennessee. He was a lawyer and a newspaper editor.

In December 1834, Childress went to Texas. His uncle, Sterling Robertson, was starting a colony near the Brazos River. Childress liked what he saw.

The Texas Revolution had already started when Childress moved to Robertson's Colony. At this time, the General Council governed Texas. In February, the General Council called a meeting. Each **province** sent men to the meeting. Sterling Robertson and George Childress were sent to represent their province, Viesca (beeYES-kah).

The meeting began on March 1, 1836, at Washington-on-the-Brazos. On the first day of the meeting, Childress presented a **resolution**, or statement. He wanted to write a declaration of independence. The resolution passed.

Childress wrote the declaration. It stated why Texas wanted to be free from Mexico. The role Childress played in gaining independence for Texas was like the role Thomas Jefferson played in the American Revolution.

statue of George Childress holding the Texas Declaration of Independence

Texas Declaration of Independence

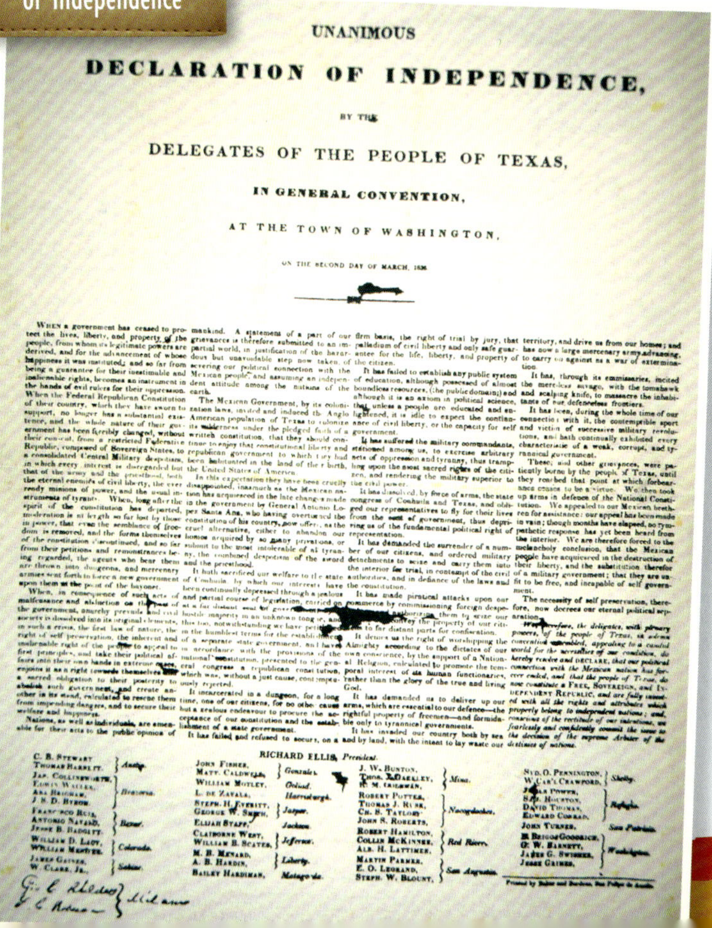

UNANIMOUS

DECLARATION OF INDEPENDENCE,

BY THE

DELEGATES OF THE PEOPLE OF TEXAS,

IN GENERAL CONVENTION,

AT THE TOWN OF WASHINGTON,

ON THE SECOND DAY OF MARCH, 1836.

Robertson's Colony

When Sterling Robertson came to Texas, the Law of April 6, 1830 had just been passed. The law prevented American settlers from coming to Texas. Robertson and his colonists settled in Austin's Colony. In 1834, Robertson was granted a new land contract. He created Robertson's Colony. After the Texas Revolution, Robertson's Colony was divided into 30 counties.

Declaration of Independence

George Childress's Texas Declaration of Independence argued that the Mexican government had violated the Mexican Constitution of 1824. It said that Texas had to separate itself from Mexico as a way to survive.

Lorenzo de Zavala

Lorenzo de Zavala (lo-REHN-soh deh sa-BAH-lah) saw many changes happen in his native Mexico. When Mexico won independence from Spain, Zavala became one of the new Mexican government's leaders. He had several jobs. He served as senator, governor, and secretary of the treasury.

Lorenzo de Zavala

Zavala wanted more **democracy** for Mexico. But many disagreed with Zavala. So he left the Mexican government.

Zavala went to New York in 1830. There, he tried to get Americans to move to Texas.

Zavala returned to Mexico in 1833. Antonio López de Santa Anna (ahn-TOH-nee-oh LOH-pehs deh SAHN-tah AH-nah) was now president of Mexico. He made Zavala the **minister** to France. But Zavala did not like Santa Anna being a **dictator**. Zavala left France and returned to Texas.

Zavala decided to support the Texan revolution. He took part in the Convention of 1836. It was there that he helped write the **Constitution** of the Republic of Texas.

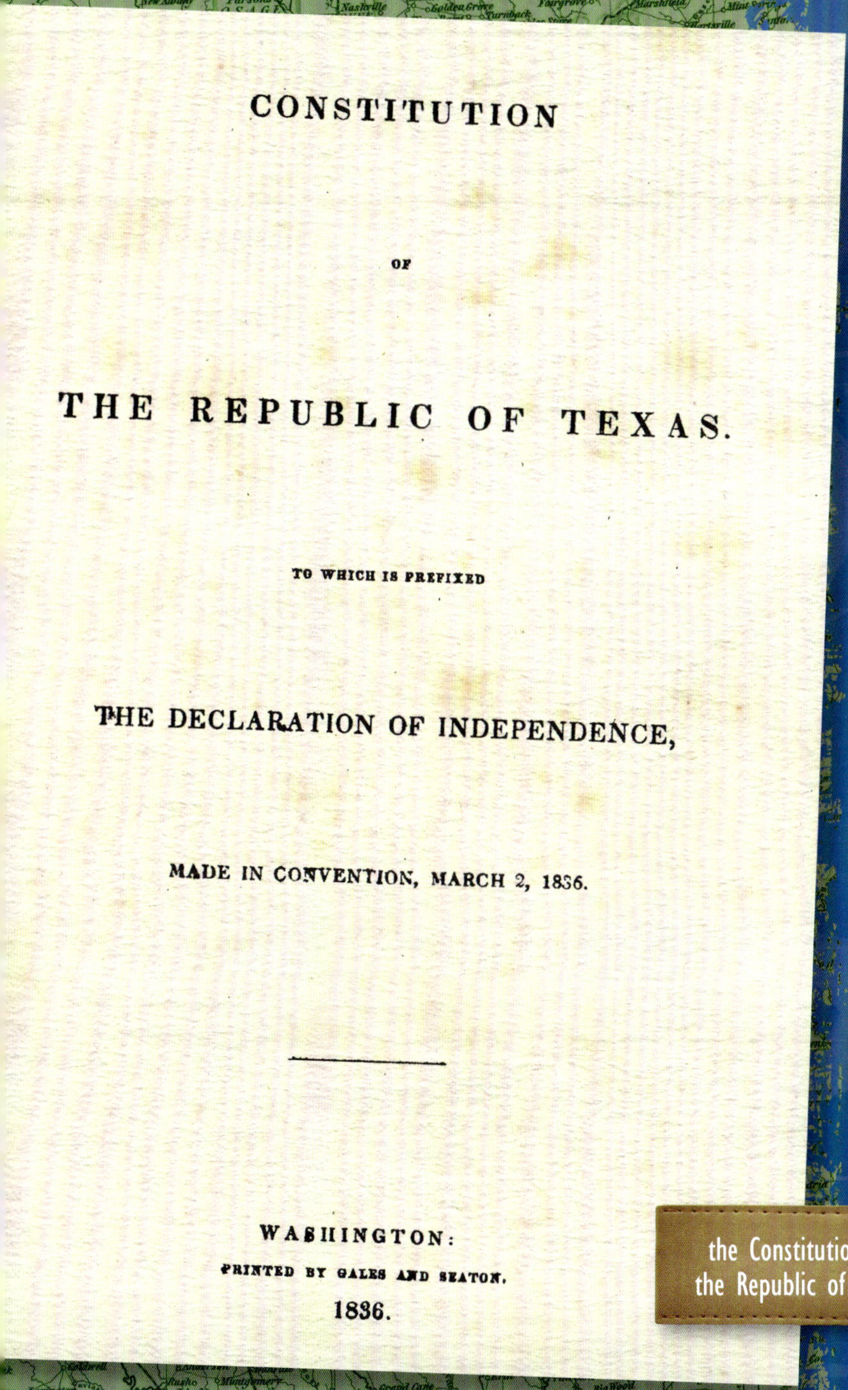

CONSTITUTION

OF

THE REPUBLIC OF TEXAS.

TO WHICH IS PREFIXED

THE DECLARATION OF INDEPENDENCE,

MADE IN CONVENTION, MARCH 2, 1836.

WASHINGTON:

PRINTED BY GALES AND SEATON.

1836.

the Constitution of the Republic of Texas

The Texas Constitution

The men who attended the Convention of 1836 wrote the first constitution for the Republic of Texas. Because of his experience, Zavala was well qualified to help write the Constitution. His peers respected Zavala and trusted his ideas. They even elected him to be the first vice president of the Republic of Texas!

The Peace Commissioner

After the Texas Revolution, Zavala was given another important job. He was a peace commissioner. It was his job to take the captured Santa Anna back to Mexico City. Santa Anna was to convince the Mexican leaders to accept Texas independence.

Defenders of the Alamo

William B. Travis

William B. Travis was a lawyer. He was also a newspaper publisher from Alabama. Travis made his way to Texas in 1831. He set up a law practice, but it was not very successful.

When fighting broke out in Texas, Travis wanted to help. He arrived too late to join the fight in Gonzales. So Travis joined the **militia** (mi-LISH-uh). It was his job to find men for the army.

In January 1836, Travis was sent to San Antonio. Santa Anna and the Mexican Army were heading to San Antonio to stop the Texas rebellion. Travis was put in charge of the troops at the Alamo. Travis knew he and his men would be outnumbered, so he wrote letters asking the United States for help.

William B. Travis

The Mexican Army attacked the Alamo on March 6, 1836. They overpowered Travis and his men in a few hours. Nearly all the men died, but their courage inspired other men to join the fight for independence.

Travis and volunteers at the Alamo

Travis's Letter

On February 24, 1836, William B. Travis was in charge of Texas troops at the Alamo. The Mexican army was about to attack. Travis wrote a letter addressed "To the People of Texas" asking for their help:

...I shall never surrender or retreat. I call on you in the name of liberty, of patriotism and everything dear to the American character to come to our aid with all dispatch. . . Victory or death.

According to legend, Travis used his sword to draw a line in the sand before the Alamo battle. He is said to have asked the Texans there to cross the line if they were willing to die with him. But historians think this story is false.

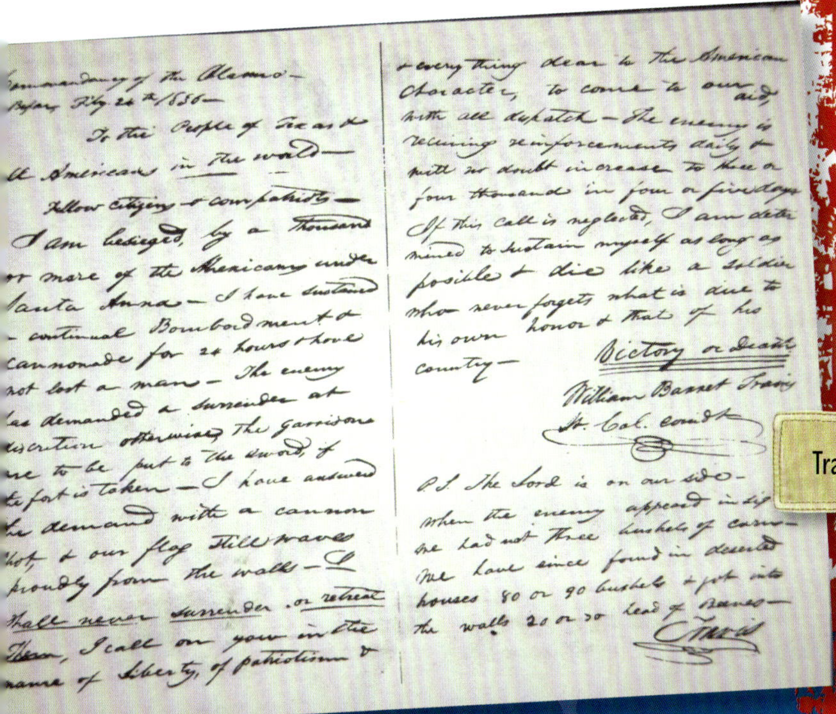

ommandancy of the Alamo—
ejar Fby 24th 1836—
To the People of Texas &
ll Americans in the world—
Fellow citizens & compatriots—
I am besieged, by a thousand
or more of the Mexicans under
anta Anna — I have sustained
continual Bombardment &
cannonade for 24 hours & have
not lost a man — The enemy
has demanded a surrender at
iscretion, otherwise, the garrison
re to be put to the sword, if
he fort is taken — I have answered
he demand with a cannon
hot, & our flag still waves
proudly from the walls — I
hall never surrender or retreat
Then, I call on you in the
name of Liberty, of patriotism &
everything dear to the American
character, to come to our aid,
with all dispatch — The enemy is
receiving reinforcements daily &
will no doubt increase to three or
four thousand in four or five days.
If this call is neglected, I am deter-
mined to sustain myself as long as
possible & die like a soldier
who never forgets what is due to
his own honor & that of his
country — Victory or Death
William Barret Travis
Lt. Col. comdt

P.S. The Lord is on our side—
When the enemy appeared in sight
we had not three bushels of corn—
We have since found in deserted
houses 80 or 90 bushels & got into
the walls 20 or 30 head of Beeves—
Travis

Travis's letter

James Bowie

James Bowie

James Bowie (BOH-ee) was a restless young man. He loved adventure and the outdoors. He liked trapping bears and riding alligators. He was often involved in gunfights and **duels**. He was also known to be a skilled knife fighter.

In 1830, Bowie went to Texas looking for adventure. He also wanted new ways to make money. He married into a powerful Mexican family. In September 1835, Stephen F. Austin was forming an army. Bowie joined.

the fall of the Alamo

Bowie knife

Bowie was in many of the battles of the Texas Revolution. He led a group of soldiers at the Battle of Concepción (kohn-sep-SEEOHN). Later, he led soldiers in the Grass Fight.

In February 1836, Sam Houston sent Bowie to the Alamo. Houston told Bowie to destroy the Alamo. But Bowie decided to defend it. During the attack, Bowie was shot to death.

Bowie Knife

James Bowie's knife became part of his legend. He was said to have owned a large butcher knife. Bowie used this knife to hunt and defend himself. Those who saw Bowie use the knife went to knife makers and asked for one like his. The knife became known as a *Bowie knife*.

Carlos Espalier

Somewhere between 189 and 257 defenders of the Alamo died during the battle. Of this group, only six were actually born in Texas. One of them was Carlos Espalier (ehs-pal-ee-EH). He was 17 years old when he died defending the Alamo. Bowie is said to have taken Espalier under his wing to teach him how to be a strong fighter and leader.

David Crockett

David Crockett was born in Tennessee in 1786. He was hardworking and loved adventure. He fought in the Creek Indian War and in the War of 1812.

Crockett was a **frontiersman**, a hunter, and a **sharpshooter**. He enjoyed telling stories about his adventures. Many stories were published about Crockett.

Actor Fess Parker portrayed David Crockett on television.

Crockett tells his famous stories to a crowd.

In 1827, Crockett was elected to the United States **House of Representatives**. But in 1834, he lost his job in Congress. Crockett decided to go to Texas. In a letter to a friend, Crockett wrote that he hoped to get rich and be a leader in Texas.

In January 1836, Crockett joined the fight for independence. In February, Crockett went to the Alamo. Soon after he arrived, Santa Anna attacked. Crockett fought bravely defending the Alamo. But he did not survive the battle.

Crockett at the Alamo

Crockett died outside the Alamo. Many people have wondered why he was found outside. Since most people at the Alamo died, there was no one to tell what had happened to Crockett. Some believe that he survived the attack but was later put to death by Santa Anna outside the fort.

The Last Survivor

Seven-year-old Enrique Esparza was in the Alamo during the attack. He saw many Texans die during the battle, including his father. By the early 1900s, Esparza was the only living survivor of the battle. He helped tell the story of the Alamo until he died in 1917. He said that he could never forget what happened at the Alamo because it was such a horrible scene.

Women of the Revolution

Susanna Dickinson

Susanna Dickinson came to Texas with her husband in 1831. The Dickinsons settled in DeWitt's Colony near Gonzales.

In October 1835, the first battle of the Texas Revolution took place in Gonzales. People think that Susanna hid in the woods with her daughter during the fight. After the battle, her husband Almaron (ahl-muh-ROHN) went with Stephen F. Austin to defend San Antonio. In December, Susanna and her daughter, Angelina, joined Almaron at the Alamo.

Susanna Dickinson

the Alamo

Texans defend the Alamo.

Almost every Texan at the Alamo died in the fight. Almaron died there, too. But Susanna and her daughter survived. They were taken to Santa Anna. Susanna tried to convince him to let her and her daughter live. He gave them two dollars in silver and a blanket. He sent them to Sam Houston with a letter warning Houston to stop fighting or die.

Texas was a hard place for single women. Dickinson was young and had a child. She could not read or write. But she was a strong woman who wanted to give her daughter a good life. She later remarried and moved to Austin. She lived there until her death in 1883.

Alamo Non-Combatants

The Battle of the Alamo was violent and deadly. All of the Texan soldiers were killed. Santa Anna lost around 600 Mexican soldiers. There were about 20 women, children, and slaves in the Alamo when the battle took place. They were considered to be "non-combatants." This means they were not involved in fighting. Santa Anna released them when the fighting was over.

Francita Alavez

Francita Alavez (frahn-SEE-tah ah-lah-BEHS) helped many soldiers during the Texas Revolution. Not much is known about her. Some think she was the wife of a Mexican Army officer. Many said she helped sick and injured soldiers. They also said she saved many lives.

Francita Alavez traveled with Captain Alavez of the Mexican Army. Wherever she went, people told stories of her kind deeds. At Copano (KOH-puh-no) Bay, she saw prisoners tightly bound with ropes. She asked the Mexican soldiers to loosen the ropes. They did what she asked.

statue of Francita Alavez

Goliad Fort where the Goliad Massacre occurred

Some stories say that Alavez was at the Goliad (GO-lee-ad) Massacre. They say she helped the prisoners there. She also helped soldiers at the Battle of San Jacinto.

Because of her kind deeds, Francita Alavez was a true hero of the Texas Revolution.

Angel of Goliad

Nobody knows Francita Alavez's real name. People thought she was Captain Alavez's wife because she traveled with him. So they called her Francita Alavez. But she was not his wife. Most people today know her as the Angel of Goliad for her kind deeds.

Doctors in the Texas Revolution

Many American doctors came to Texas to help during the revolution. They lived and died beside those who fought. Sometimes, doctors were taken prisoner by the Mexican Army so they could help Mexican soldiers.

Choosing Sides

Plácido Benavides

Plácido Benavides (PLAH-see-doh beh-nah-BEE-dehs) was a **Tejano** (tay-HA-ṇo) landowner. *Tejano* means a Texan of Mexican **heritage**. He was also an **alcalde** (ahl-KAHL-dey), or city official. Benavides was a loyal Mexican who did not support independence for Texas. But Benavides believed that Santa Anna was his enemy.

Benavides helped to defend Texas against the Mexican Army. After the Battle of Gonzales, he helped train the new volunteers who joined the fight for independence. Benavides also fought in the Siege of Bexar (BEH-har). He was recognized for his bravery and hard work.

map of the Alamo area in San Antonio based on Santa Anna's original battlefield map in Spanish

Santa Anna

In 1836, Benavides learned of Santa Anna's plan to trap the Texans in Goliad and Bexar. He warned Robert Morris, the officer in charge. That warning was sent to others who were able to prepare for Santa Anna's attack.

Benavides felt divided between Mexico and Texas. He returned to his ranch and tried to stay out of the conflict.

The Paul Revere of Texas

When Benavides found out about Santa Anna's plan at Goliad, he rode through Goliad and Victoria to warn people that the Mexicans were coming. This earned him the nickname, Paul Revere of Texas. Revere warned patriots that the British troops were coming during the American Revolution.

Traitor!

Many Tejanos, like Benavides, were considered traitors by both sides in the conflict. Other Tejanos believed that Benavides did not do all he could to protect their interests in Texas. He and his family had to leave Texas for New Orleans, where he died in 1837.

Juan Seguín

a battle during the Mexican-American War

Juan Seguín

As a Mexican, Juan Seguín (wahn seh-GEEN) was loyal to his country. But as a Texan, he wanted independence from Mexico. He did not like the harsh rule of Santa Anna.

In 1835, Seguín led a militia group in the fight against Santa Anna. He was made a captain because of his role in the Battle of Gonzales.

Seguín brought his soldiers to the Alamo. But he was sent away on a mission. He went to **recruit** more men to fight for Texas independence. While Seguín was away, the Mexican Army attacked the Alamo.

Seguín was not happy with the Texans' behavior after the revolution. He felt like a foreigner, or stranger, in his own country. So Seguín left Texas for Mexico in 1842.

Tejano

Seguín led the only Tejano regiment in the Battle of San Jacinto. The population of Texas has always been diverse. Over time, American Indians, Mexicans, and **Anglo-Americans** have identified themselves as Texans.

The Mexican-American War

Seguín fought for Mexico in the Mexican-American War. Texas was made a part of the United States in 1845. In 1846, war broke out between the United States and Mexico over the boundary between the two nations and the American desire to claim more Mexican land. When the war ended in 1848, the Rio Grande was recognized as the border, and the United States gained a large amount of territory.

Professional Soldier

James Fannin

James Fannin

James Fannin was one of the few Texans who was trained as a professional soldier. He attended the United States Military Academy at West Point, New York.

In 1834, Fannin moved to Velasco (beh-LAHS-koh), Texas. Like some others who came to Texas, Fannin was a **plantation** owner and a slave trader. Fannin wanted independence from Mexico. He asked West Point officers to come to Texas and fight. He also asked people to send money for the cause.

Fannin was captain of the Brazos Guards at the Battle of Gonzales. Along with James Bowie, he led the forces at the Battle of Concepción.

students at the United States Military Academy at West Point

Sam Houston made Fannin a commander of the army at Goliad. At Goliad, Fannin made several big mistakes. The Mexican Army surrounded Fannin and his men. They forced them to **surrender**. On March 27, 1835, Santa Anna ordered Fannin and nearly 350 men to be shot to death. The Goliad Massacre made many Americans angry.

West Point

The United States Military Academy at West Point is a place where men and women can receive a college education and prepare for service in the U.S. Army. West Point has been used for military training since the American Revolution.

Big Mistakes

Fannin was not a perfect leader. His professional military background did not fit well with his volunteer soldiers. Many of his soldiers did not like him. Before Goliad, Fannin even asked to be replaced as leader of his troops. But despite his mistakes, Fannin fought bravely for Texas independence.

Battle of San Jacinto

"Remember the Alamo!"

Sidney Sherman

Sidney Sherman learned early in life how to take care of himself. He was born in Massachusetts in 1805. He became an orphan at age 12. Sherman was smart and hardworking. In 1835, Sherman decided to move to Texas. Before he moved, he recruited Texans to fight for independence.

When Sherman and his men reached Texas, Sam Houston made him an army leader. At the Battle of San Jacinto, Sherman led the attack on the second day. Many believe he was the first to call out to his men "Remember the Alamo!" Sherman hoped his men would think of those who had already lost their lives in the fight for Texas independence. He believed that would help his men fight bravely in their honor.

Sherman was one of the many men and women who led Texas through the revolution. They fought in battles, nursed the injured, and gave their lives for Texas independence. Their stories still inspire Texans.

Sidney Sherman

Many Tragedies

Sidney Sherman faced many tragedies during his life. His home and office burned down several times. In 1852, Sherman was on the steamer ship *Farmer* when it exploded. He hung onto a piece of the wreckage until he was rescued. And Sherman's son was killed at the Battle of Galveston during the Civil War.

Remember the Alamo

Men who fought in the Texas Revolution used the Battle of the Alamo as a rallying cry. As they charged Santa Anna at the Battle of San Jacinto, they called out, "Remember the Alamo!"

Glossary

alcalde—the mayor or chief judge of a town

Anglo-Americans—white Americans of European descent

colonization—the act or process of forming colonies

constitution—a written statement outlining the basic laws for a state or country

democracy—ability for the people to have a say in government

dictator—a person who has absolute power

duels—fights between two people

empresario—a person given a land grant by the Mexican government to make a settlement and recruit people to live there

frontiersman—a person who lives on the frontier

heritage—tradition and culture passed down at birth

House of Representatives—a group of elected officials who have the power to make and pass laws

militia—a group of citizen soldiers

minister—a government representative in a foreign country

plantation—a type of large farm found in the southern United States

province—a district or region of a territory

recruit—to select or get the services of someone

resolution—a formal expression of opinion

revolution—an act of overthrowing and replacing one government with another

sharpshooter—a person skilled in shooting a gun

surrender—to give up

Tejano—a Mexican-born Texan

Texians—people living in Mexican Texas between 1821 and 1836

Index

Your Turn!

There were many heroes of the Texas Revolution. Some of them fought bravely. Others wrote important documents. Francita Alavez was different. No one knows much about her, not even her real name! She traveled with the Mexican Army, but she helped many Texan soldiers. She nursed the wounded and made sure Texan prisoners were treated humanely.

Lyrics for a Legend

Write a song about the legendary kindness of Francita Alavez. Set your lyrics to a familiar tune.